BUTTERFLY

Published by Spines
ISBN: 979-8-89569-189-2

BUTTERFLY

BETH SARVER ASHWORTH

CONTENTS

CHAPTER 1
THE JOURNEY

There is cold dew on the grass, and the trees are full of leafy green goodness. I think that it is springtime! There is a familiar feeling in the air... like I have been here before. I instinctively know that I must be extra careful to shield myself from the birds flying in the sky. I am their favorite treat!

As I inch my way under a hanging leaf on the old oak tree, I look around and can tell that this is the perfect place to stop. I can hardly wait to dig into the leaves. As I bow my head and open my small mouth to take my very first bite, there is a sudden and strong gust of wind.

The wind is strong enough to sweep me up and hurl me to the wet ground below. The branches are now so far away from where I am. I must climb back up the old oak tree.

Right now, I only have one goal: to eat enough so I can grow as much as needed for my journey ahead.

Finally, after the challenging work of inching my way back to the oak tree's lowest branches... I can calm my growing hunger. I position myself under one of the leaves to provide shelter from the wind, far from the view of the many birds soaring above, looking for a juicy snack.

As I am finishing my very first leaf, I can see the sun setting in the west sky. I eagerly await the arrival of the moon. This is when I am most alive and full of vigorous energy.

I use this time to consume as much as I can because, as the sky brightens and the sun rises, I will become ever more vulnerable. The new day will light the way for more predators. I risk being the worm that the early birds were promised.

I will need to find a cozy nook and burrow deep so that I can stay safe. I like to get my rest when the sun is passing in the sky.

As I inch my way to the leaf that is most suitable for shelter, my eyelids become oh so heavy.

Yes, this is a nice cozy hideaway. I do believe I will be safe here for the latter part of the day. I will rest here until sunset.

CHAPTER 2
A FLUTTER OF HOPE

As I rest lightly to regain my strength, I can hear the screeching cries of hatchlings three branches up above. Their cries of hunger are ear-curdling screeches. It was all that I could hear. It occurred to me that their mother must be on a hunt for food. Then it occurred to me that I am exactly what she would be looking for! With this thought, I burrowed back just a little further into the tight notch under the leaf for secure shelter.

I watched and listened as the mother of the hatchlings swooped in towards the big oak tree, with a very loud screech to warn off any potential predators. In her mouth is a big juicy silkworm. She dives directly towards her nest and grabs one of the outer branches with her extraordinarily strong and sharp talons.

She is only there to regurgitate the silkworm. She does this to create a suitable texture for her young. Next, she will spit it into the mouths of her hatchlings before she flies away. Her wings stretch from side to side, allowing the wind to do most of the work for her. It is still and quiet for a moment, allowing me to drift off once again, fast asleep.

The sun sets again, bringing in the cool and breezy night. The moon returns to its usual position in the sky, and I can feel my tiny tummy growling at me. My hunger expresses an urgency to consume the foliage that surrounds me. So, I did. Milkweed is my favorite.

Each day and night passed as the ones before, and things around me were beginning to change... including myself! My long and hairy exoskeleton and all my suction cups began to get tight, and just when I thought that my body could not take any more, boom, it happened!

I began to molt, and I shed my head capsule. As I shed

my exoskeleton, I suddenly felt comfortable once again. Then, just as before, there was a sudden and urgent need to consume everything around me. So, I did!

The crisp, crunchy oak tree leaves are also a favorite. But there are many others who are also here to consume the forage as I am.

The supply is not as plentiful as it once was weeks ago. I must be the luckiest in the entire world. Here, there is barely enough greenery to feed all the others and myself, but with my luck, I inched right into the new growth from under the demolished branches. It is best to keep this news to myself. My food intake is crucial at this stage in my journey.

As each day sets in and the nights grow to come quicker and ever so fast, another week would pass me by. I shed my exoskeleton two more times, reaching my third instar stage. Then, I noticed that my spiracles were multiplying as fast as time came and went by.

CHAPTER 3
METAMORPHOSES

Looking over to the nearest branch, I could see how little I once was and the notches that others like myself had left behind. It was then that I realized that the cool and breezy branches would forever be a pleasant reminder of my past.

Then... suddenly out of nowhere, it hit me like a June bug, right in the head; It is now time for me to spin a button nautch on the underneath of a leaf hanging from the branch of the old Oak tree.

Somewhere that will provide long term shelter and stability. This chosen destination must be capable of sustaining all the weather possibilities and protect me from predators during my time as a chrysalis.

I have the perfect spot figured out. I believe that my time to chrysalis is coming near. Now I am spending most, if not all, my time consuming the green leaves that surround me. As another sweltering day and long night pass me by, I reach my fourth and fifth instar stages. It is now time to spin my button or (pupate). I have completed metamorphosis!

I will now spend the next 10 to 14 days as a pupa or (chrysalis). When I appear from the dark and lonely cocoon, I will be female. I will use my beauty and vast colors to attract a male, then I will lay my eggs on the old oak tree just as my mother did for my siblings and me.

Oh, how I just love this old oak tree! As I took the time to settle in and get comfortable and cozy, I started to close my eyes. It was rest that was very much needed, and I was excited to catch up.

Twelve days passed by as I slept comfortably in my

very well-spun cocoon. I started to hear the very loud and high-pitched voices of children playing beneath the high branches of the oak tree!

As I slowly remembered who I am and what I am, I realized that my cocoon had become extremely thin, and I could see the rambunctious children playing beneath the oak tree.

I got excited to have been awakened. Now it is time for me to appear, as I have been waiting for this very moment for so long. My whole journey up until now has been all about this incredibly special moment.

I can hardly wait to spread my wings and fly, for I am now a butterfly. Oh, what a magnificent feeling of being free! My wings are so beautiful. I can hardly concentrate on the world around me.

Okay, steady, steady; steady now, wings. Okay, I think, I think I can do this. And I am off into the beautiful, vast world of many possibilities. Now I must drink the sweet nectar of the many different-colored flowers and do my part to help pollinate the earth.

You see, as I fly down to drink the sweet nectar, the pollen will stick to my wings and my body. Then, as I fly away, the pollen drops from my wings onto the ground, allowing fresh flowers to grow.

CHAPTER 4

SECRETS WITHIN THE GARDEN

But there is something that keeps my attention away from the flowers. I cannot really seem to focus. He is so beautiful, but I am not yet ready for a mate. I have not yet reached my imago stage.

By the time spring comes, I will be ready, and I think I have found the perfect mate. Wait, oh, I think he—he is noticing me. He is flying my way.

"Excuse me, miss," he says, "hello, I am Mark the monarch, and I was wondering, are you going to join the great monarch migration at the end of this week?" he asked me with a strong, confident voice.

But I had never heard of this great migration that he had spoken of, so I replied, "Hello, Mark the monarch."

"I am, I am, I am; well, I guess I do not have a name," she replied in her very adorable, nervous, and shaky voice.

"I guess nobody has named me yet. But about this migration, I am sorry, could you please explain?"

"Well, if you do not mind, I would like to call you Daisy. I could not help but notice your vibrant and extraordinarily beautiful colors, and I noticed your harmonic aroma as soon as I came close to you! You remind me of a breathtaking flower, a daisy to be exact."

Then, with hope and inspiration, Mark let Daisy know that everyone would be leaving in just a few days. He then asked her if she would like to be his flying partner, and Daisy quickly replied without hesitation that she would be delighted to be his flying partner and was looking forward to getting to know him on a more personal level.

As the days passed and the migration came near, all Daisy could think about was how wonderful it was going to be to join the great migration with Mark, who she had already made friends with.

As Daisy sat with anticipation, she found herself daydreaming about the migration. Will the others like her as Mark did? Daisy thought to herself.

Daisy started to get more nervous as time ticked by, and with only one more day ahead before the migration, she started to get cold feet and was extremely nervous.

Daisy's tummy was rolling with excitement, and she just could not bring herself to go through with the migration. Maybe if she had met everyone beforehand, or even just a few others, only then would she feel comfortable, Daisy thought tirelessly.

As Daisy talked herself in and out of the migration jour-ney, she suddenly noticed the deep vibration of many wings coming her way. Daisy quickly recognized that this was the sound of butterfly wings in sequence.

CHAPTER 5
THE GREAT MIGRATION

Her heart dropped to her stomach, and her face felt all red with flush. The sound grew closer and closer, and she could hardly keep herself from fainting. Before she could swallow the lump that rested within her throat, there he stood. It was Mark the monarch, and he had come to collect Daisy for her spot in the great migration.

"Come on, Daisy," he said, "it is time for the great migration, and I have saved a special spot just for you. Everyone is so excited and cannot wait to meet you. I have told them how beautiful and wonderful you are. I have also let them know how special you are to me."

Daisy, in that moment, was paralyzed. She was struck by Mark's presence. Mark gently tugged at Daisy's wings to guide her in the direction of the rest of the monarchs. Daisy could not speak as she followed Mark's direction, and with her mouth sealed and her heart heavy, Daisy began to fly.

The monarchs flew and they flew and they flew. It was like they were born to fly, and nothing else mattered. Close to Mark's side, they flew 2,551 miles from Canada all the way to Mexico. This happened year after year so that they could wait out the chilly winter, only to fly directly back the next spring.

Daisy started to show signs of exertion, and her mouth was so dry. Then, right when the feeling of giving up crossed her mind, Mark let out an exciting and electrifying scream, "Whoo-hoo, we made it, everyone! We did it, we finally made it! Just over those hills, and then we can finally taste the sweetness in the air that my mother once told me about."

As they flew over the hills, they were met with such a different feeling in the atmosphere. The flowers—you could taste them in the air. Oh, what a magnificent sight to see. The ground was completely covered with milkweed and poinsettias. The vibrant colors were so bright they were almost blinding. Daisy could hardly wait as she set out for her long-anticipated landing.

Daisy could not help but dream of the days to come. What a perfect place to frolic with friends, she thought quietly to herself. Everything was perfect in that moment as Daisy, Mark, and the others indulged in the beautiful valley completely covered with the cool, crisp, and sweet nectar that surrounded them.

The great monarch migration is essential to the rebirth and future development of Mexico's terrain. Butterflies are highly depended on to fly all the way across the eastern sky every year from Canada into Mexico during the winter.

It is the butterfly that is alongside the bumblebee and honeybee, overseeing the pollination of many diverse types of fruit, flowers, plants, and trees.

CHAPTER 6

SAVING DAISY

As Daisy and Mark frolic from plant to plant, all that Daisy could think about was how it was going to be so great to lay her eggs back in the old oak tree. Mesmerized by the scene of nature that surrounded her, she lost sight of all the others.

She knew that they could not have gone too far away and continued to drink the sweet nectar from the beautiful flowers. It was quiet for a moment until suddenly, she heard a loud thump on one of the leaves next to her.

Daisy looked all around with excitement, only to be disappointed that she could not find the source of the thump. It had to come from somewhere, but where? About that time, she could hear the faint voice of Mark in the distance coming towards her. He was calling her name, "Daisy, Daisy, where are you?"

Then suddenly, there was another thump, but this time it was even closer than before. Almost like it was coming after her. Daisy moved over to the left just a little to see if the thump followed. As Mark got closer to where Daisy was, she let out a loud, "Mark, I am over here," so that he could pinpoint her location. As he spotted her, there was another thump, and just as Daisy had suspected, it had indeed followed her.

Mark landed on a pedal from the flower next to Daisy. He quickly noticed something frightening. He tried to get Daisy's attention without being too obvious. Mark, flapping his wings with intent and determination, could not get Daisy's attention. As Daisy turned to talk to Mark, she could tell that he was distraught with fear. She could not quite understand what was going on.

Mark kept an eye on the big green and purple giant and saw as it changed from one color to another. It was like it was part of the plant, but he knew better. About this time, he could see a huge lump in the giant's throat rising slowly, and he knew he had to get Daisy out of harm's way. So, he rose up and took flight right into the side of Daisy.

Daisy and Mark both tumbled onto the hard ground as the giant unrolled his extra-long tongue and aimed at the very spot where Daisy was before Mark pushed her onto the hard ground. It was then that it became clear that this giant was trying to eat Daisy. Mark quickly explained his motive for his actions as Daisy listened in pain.

"Daisy, are you okay?" asked Mark. "That giant chameleon was trying to eat you," he said with hesitation in his voice. "I do apologize to you, my sweet Daisy, but I had to save you."

Although she was very thankful, one of her wings was damaged from the rubble below, and Daisy was quite hurt. In fact, this was going to put her out of commission for days, if not weeks. Daisy needed time to heal.

Mark worked fast to build a soft and comfortable place for Daisy, as she would need to heal. He then carried Daisy as he flew her over to her newly built shelter. Mark did all he could do to keep her comfortable for the coming days that lay ahead.

Every day, Mark did everything he could think of to keep Daisy comfortable and safe. He gathered sweet nectar every day for almost two weeks. He assured Daisy that he would always be by her side to protect her and keep her safe. Mark promised Daisy that she could always count on him.

CHAPTER 7

THE RECOVERY

As the days continued to go by, even the other butterflies chipped in to do their part, collecting nectar to bring back to Daisy so she could have the strength she needed to heal. It was a team effort, and working together seemed to pay off because, before they knew it, Daisy was expressing the need to fly once again.

"I am ready," said Daisy to Mark with excitement! "Are you sure?" said Mark. "You know, there is no rush, Daisy. We don't mind picking up the slack so you can heal. Take all the time that you need." But Daisy, in a determined voice, assured Mark that she was ready. So together they walked out to the edge of the branches, and just before Daisy could take flight, Mark reminded her that if she felt the need to change her mind or if the pain was too much, not to hesitate to try again later, allowing more time for her to heal.

Daisy, in her confident voice, assured Mark and the others that she knew what she was doing and that she was ready. She then stretched her wings, and at that very moment, Daisy felt a very slight sense of pain. But Daisy was strong, and she pushed through. She leaped with intent, and before she knew it, she was flying once again. The sense of being free was stronger than the pain, and the sweet nectar replaced the painful sensation with a sense of fulfillment.

The time to fly back to Canada was growing near. Daisy thought it would be wise to set Mark down and have a chat with him. Daisy wanted to include Mark in her plans to lay her eggs back home in the old oak tree. Daisy set off to find Mark, and after a while, she was able to find him.

But something was not right. Her hands were all sweaty, her heart was beating fast, her tummy was rolling with excitement, and there were lumps in her throat. She could hardly speak. "Hey Daisy, what a pleasant surprise," said Mark, as he laid his eyes upon Daisy when she came his way.

"Hey Mark," Daisy replied, with a sense of nervous energy that was obviously radiating from her. "What's wrong, Daisy? You look a little flushed," Mark said. "Is everything okay?" he asked her with a concerned look on his face. Daisy replied, "Everything's okay, Mark. I just really wanted to talk to you about something." "Okay, Daisy, what is that?" said Mark. "Well, I really do not know if I should."

"It's okay, Daisy. Remember, you can speak to me about anything. I am here for you always. Nothing you say to me can be wrong." "Well, okay if you insist, Mark," said Daisy. "Okay, well, let's have it. What do you have to say?" said Mark, as he stared with intent into her eyes.

"Well, I was wondering if you would be interested in helping me pollinate so that I can lay my eggs back in the old oak tree, where I was born?" "Are you asking me if I would like to father your young?" said Mark with excitement. "Well, yes," Daisy replied. "As a matter of fact, I am. It's just that I have not really felt close to anyone but you. I believe we have a strong connection. Our offspring would be like no other. I guess what I am trying to say is, I think you're the perfect match for me."

Mark's eyes lit up with a sense of willingness as he quickly replied, "I would be delighted, Daisy. As a matter of fact, I was going to ask you if you had found a mate."

As a few more days passed and everyone slowed from devouring the sweet nectar that surrounded them, the time to get their rest for the trip home was growing near. All Daisy could think about was her natural instinct to reproduce. As though there was a timer on her clock of life, the urge grew stronger and stronger until finally, it was time. Everyone gathered in the valley to create a beautiful blanket of monarchs.

They were off on their journey to migrate back towards Canada. Daisy and Mark flew side by side, never drifting too far apart. They even had various deep conversations about one another and what they wanted out of life. No butterfly knew any other butterfly better than Daisy and Mark. They were two peas in a pod, and nothing in this world could tear them apart.

CHAPTER 8

A FAMILIAR PLACE

A couple of days passed as they continued flying. Realizing that they were just a little over halfway to their destination, Daisy felt a sense of relief knowing that she was almost to the old oak tree. It was then that she knew everything was going to be fine. Daisy began to let her guard down, allowing her eyes to drift closed for extended periods of time as the wind caught her wings to do the flying for her. Mark noticed that Daisy was growing tired and allowed her to rest on his back as he flew for them both. Daisy could then feel herself growing weaker and weaker as the old oak tree came closer and closer.

She could not understand why this sudden overwhelming tiredness had taken over her. She could not help but feel that something just was not right. It was taking all her strength just to keep her eyes open. She could not understand but could feel that something was terribly wrong. She expressed an urgency to Mark that she needed to get to the old oak tree as soon as possible because something was not right.

Mark flapped his wings faster and faster, doing everything he could to get Daisy to the old oak tree so that she could lay their eggs. "I'm going as fast as I can," said Mark. "I promise you, Daisy, I will get you there. Just close your eyes and try to relax." "I can't close my eyes. I feel as though I am not going to make it," said Daisy. With a sense of uncertainty, Mark was filled with sadness. He expressed to Daisy that she had to keep going.

She had to make it to the old oak tree. "I do not know if I can," said Daisy. "I am just going to lay my eggs here." "No, Daisy," said Mark. "You have to make it to the old oak tree. This is what you've always wanted. I will make sure you get there. Just stay with me."

After a few more hours of flying, Mark, with excitement, let Daisy know that they were coming near the old oak tree. Expecting a response, Mark heard nothing. "Daisy, are you there? Are you awake?" "Daisy!" said Mark. There was no reply. Mark flew just a little faster and then a little faster as he could not flap his wings any faster. Then he noticed he had the old oak tree in his sight.

"We are here! We made it! We're at the old oak tree!" "Come on, you have to wake up!" He could hear Daisy faintly breathing as her eyes began slowly to open. "Mark," said Daisy with weakness, "if I am going to lay our eggs here, I am going to need you to hurry and gather everything you can to make something soft, cozy, and comfortable for the eggs. It must shield them from predators." Mark then let Daisy know that he would be back with everything he needed to create the nest.

Deep down inside, Mark knew that he had no idea what he was doing or where to even start. Mark then moved quickly, gathering everything he thought he would need. Mark knew he was doing the best job he possibly could. He then returned to Daisy's side. Then he began to build the nest, and as Mark finished with the final touches, he encouraged Daisy to lay her eggs.

Daisy was very weak; it took all she had to lay her eggs. Mark could tell from Daisy's condition that something was terribly wrong. Although he was incredibly sad, it brought him extraordinary joy to know that she would live on through their young. As Mark gently touched Daisy's nose with his own, giving her butterfly kisses, she took her last breath.

A few weeks would pass, and as the eggs hatched from their egg form to larvae, you could hear a very tiny voice coming from one of the larvae: "It is springtime. There is a familiar feeling in the air, like I have been here before." And just like that, a complete circle of life had formed.

The End